Sizzling Seafood Delights

A Guide to Mastering Grilled Fish

SIZZLING SEAFOOD DELIGHTS

First edition. January 3, 2024.

ISBN: 979-8224361816

Written by Jose Maria.

Table of Contents

Jose Maria

❖ Introduction

A. The Art of Grilling Fish

Grilling fish is not just a cooking technique; it's an art that brings out the natural flavors of seafood, creating a delightful and healthy culinary experience. Whether you're a seasoned griller or a novice, mastering the art of grilling fish opens up a world of delicious possibilities.

Benefits of Grilling Fish

Grilling fish offers numerous benefits, making it a popular and nutritious cooking method. Some key advantages include:

a. Healthier Option: Grilling requires minimal added fats, making it a healthier choice compared to other cooking methods.

b. Flavor Infusion: Grilling enhances the natural flavors of fish, creating a smoky, savory profile that's hard to replicate.

c. Quick and Convenient: Fish cooks relatively quickly on the grill, making it an ideal option for busy individuals or those seeking a speedy yet tasty meal.

d. Versatility: Grilling accommodates a wide range of fish varieties, allowing you to explore different flavors and textures.

Choosing the Right Fish for Grilling

Not all fish are created equal when it comes to grilling. Opt for varieties that hold up well on the grill and offer a succulent taste. Consider:

a. Firm Texture: Fish with a firm texture, such as salmon, swordfish, or halibut, tends to grill better without falling apart.

b. Oil Content: Fish with higher oil content, like mackerel or salmon, can withstand the heat of the grill without drying out.

c. Skin-on Options: Choosing fish with the skin intact helps retain moisture and adds a crispy texture to the finished dish.

Essential Grilling Tools and Equipment

To embark on your grilling journey, ensure you have the right tools and equipment at your disposal:

a. Quality Grill: Invest in a reliable grill—whether charcoal, gas, or electric—suited to your preferences and available space.

b. Grilling Utensils: Essential tools include tongs, a spatula, and a grill brush for effective cooking and maintenance.

c. Thermometer: A meat thermometer ensures your fish is perfectly cooked, preventing overcooking or undercooking.

d. Marinade Brushes: Brushes for applying marinades keep your fish moist and impart additional flavor.

e. Grill Baskets: These are handy for delicate fish varieties, preventing them from sticking to the grill grates.

Mastering the art of grilling fish begins with understanding these fundamentals. As you delve into the world of seafood on the grill, you'll discover endless possibilities for creating mouthwatering dishes that celebrate the freshness of the ocean.

Chapter (1) Fish Selection and Preparation

A. Selecting Fresh and Sustainable Seafood

Tips for Choosing Fresh Fish

a. Clear Eyes: When selecting whole fish, look for clear, bright eyes. Cloudy or sunken eyes may indicate less freshness.

b. Firm Flesh: Press the flesh with your finger; it should bounce back and feel firm. Avoid fish with soft or mushy spots.

c. Fresh Smell: Fresh fish should have a clean, ocean-like scent. Avoid any fish that has a strong, fishy odor.

d. Bright Gills: For whole fish, check the gills. They should be a vibrant red or pink color, not dull or brown.

e. Skin Integrity: If buying fillets, ensure the skin is intact and free from any discoloration or blemishes.

Sustainable Seafood Practices

a. Check Certifications: Look for seafood with certifications like MSC (Marine Stewardship Council) or ASC (Aquaculture Stewardship Council) to ensure sustainable sourcing.

b. Know Your Seafood Guide: Consult sustainable seafood guides to make informed choices based on the current status of fish populations.

c. Local and Seasonal Choices: Opt for locally sourced and seasonally available fish to support sustainable fishing practices.

B. Cleaning and Preparing Fish for Grilling

Gutting and Scaling

a. Gutting: Start by removing the innards. Make a small incision along the belly, and carefully scoop out the internal organs.

b. Scaling: Use a fish scaler or the back of a knife to remove scales. Work from tail to head, ensuring you scale both sides thoroughly.

Filleting and Deboning Techniques

a. Filleting: With a sharp knife, make an incision behind the gills and along the spine. Run the knife along the spine, separating the fillet from the bone.

b. Deboning: Check for pin bones using your fingers or tweezers and remove them. For larger fish, consider cutting the fillet into smaller, more manageable portions.

Marinades and Seasonings

a. Simple Marinade: Combine olive oil, lemon juice, minced garlic, and fresh herbs (such as parsley or dill) for a classic and versatile marinade.

b. Asian-Inspired Seasoning: Mix soy sauce, ginger, sesame oil, and a touch of honey for an umami-packed marinade.

c. Mediterranean Flavors: Create a marinade with olive oil, lemon zest, oregano, and a hint of crushed red pepper for a Mediterranean twist.

d. Spice Rub: Blend cayenne pepper, paprika, garlic powder, and thyme for a bold and spicy rub.

Once your fish is cleaned, filleted, and seasoned, you're ready to explore the exciting world of grilling. The next steps will guide you through the basics of grilling, ensuring your seafood delights are cooked to perfection.

Chapter (2) Grilling Basics

A. Types of Grills and Heat Sources

Charcoal Grills

Description: Charcoal grills use charcoal briquettes or lump charcoal as fuel. They provide a distinctive smoky flavor to grilled foods.

Advantages:

- **Intense heat for searing.**
- **Budget-friendly.**
- **Classic smoky flavor.**

Tips:

- **Allow charcoal to ash over before cooking.**
- **Control heat by adjusting airflow vents.**

Gas Grills

Description: Gas grills use propane or natural gas for quick and convenient cooking. They offer precise temperature control.

Advantages:

- **Fast and easy to start.**
- **Even heat distribution.**
- **Convenient temperature control.**

Tips:

- **Preheat the grill with the lid closed.**
- **Regularly check gas levels for uninterrupted cooking.**

Electric Grills

Description: Electric grills are powered by electricity, providing a clean and efficient grilling option.

Advantages:

- Indoor and outdoor use.
- No fuel or open flames.
- Easy to clean.

Tips:

- Preheat before use.
- Monitor power levels for temperature control.

B. Preheating and Temperature Control

Preheating: Allow the grill to preheat for 10-15 minutes to ensure even cooking and prevent sticking.

- Temperature Control:
- For gas grills, adjust the burner knobs.
- On charcoal grills, control temperature by adjusting vents.
- Electric grills usually have adjustable temperature settings.

C. Grilling Techniques

Direct vs. Indirect Heat

Direct Heat: Ideal for searing and cooking smaller, thinner cuts. Place food directly above the heat source.

Indirect Heat: Suitable for larger cuts or delicate fish. Place food away from the heat source, allowing for slower, more even cooking.

Smoking Fish on the Grill

Wood Chips: Soak wood chips (such as hickory or apple) in water, then place them on the charcoal or in a smoker box for gas grills.

Low and Slow: Maintain a low temperature for longer cooking times, infusing the fish with smoky flavor.

Planking and Foil-Wrapping

Planking: Soak a cedar or other food-safe wood plank in water, then place it directly on the grill. Lay the fish on the plank for a unique flavor infusion.

Foil-Wrapping: Wrap fish with herbs, spices, and aromatics in foil packets. This method steams the fish and preserves moisture.

Understanding these grilling basics and techniques sets the stage for creating perfectly grilled fish. In the next section, we'll explore a variety of mouthwatering marinades and rubs to elevate your seafood dishes.

Chapter (3) Marinades and Rubs

A.   Citrus and Herb Infusions

Citrus Herb Marinade:
  Ingredients:

- 1/4 cup olive oil
- 2 tablespoons fresh lemon juice
- 1 tablespoon orange zest
- 2 cloves garlic, minced
- 1 teaspoon dried oregano
- 1 teaspoon fresh thyme, chopped
- Salt and black pepper to taste

Instructions:

1. In a bowl, whisk together olive oil, lemon juice, orange zest, minced garlic, oregano, thyme, salt, and pepper.
2. Place your selected fish in a shallow dish and coat it evenly with the marinade.
3. Cover and refrigerate for at least 30 minutes, allowing the citrus and herbs to infuse into the fish.
4. Grill the marinated fish over medium heat until it reaches your desired doneness, brushing with extra marinade during cooking.

B. Asian-inspired Marinades
Teriyaki Glaze:
Ingredients:

- 1/2 cup soy sauce
- 1/4 cup mirin (Japanese sweet rice wine)
- 2 tablespoons honey
- 1 tablespoon rice vinegar
- 1 tablespoon sesame oil
- 2 cloves garlic, minced
- 1 teaspoon ginger, grated

Instructions:

1. In a saucepan, combine soy sauce, mirin, honey, rice vinegar, sesame oil, minced garlic, and grated ginger.
2. Simmer over medium heat until the mixture thickens into a glaze.
3. Let the teriyaki glaze cool, then use it to marinate fish for at least 1 hour.
4. Grill the marinated fish over medium-high heat, brushing with additional teriyaki glaze while cooking.

C. Mediterranean Flavors
Mediterranean Herb Marinade:
Ingredients:

- 1/3 cup extra-virgin olive oil
- 2 tablespoons fresh lemon juice
- 2 teaspoons dried oregano
- 1 teaspoon dried thyme
- 2 cloves garlic, minced
- Salt and black pepper to taste

Instructions:

1. Whisk together olive oil, lemon juice, oregano, thyme, minced garlic, salt, and pepper in a bowl.
2. Coat the fish with the Mediterranean herb marinade, ensuring an even distribution.
3. Refrigerate for at least 1 hour to allow the flavors to meld.
4. Grill the marinated fish over medium heat until it reaches your desired level of doneness.

D. Spicy and Bold Rubs
Cajun Spice Rub:
Ingredients:

- **2 teaspoons paprika**
- **1 teaspoon onion powder**
- **1 teaspoon garlic powder**
- **1 teaspoon dried thyme**
- **1/2 teaspoon cayenne pepper**
- **1/2 teaspoon black pepper**
- **1/2 teaspoon white pepper**
- **1/2 teaspoon dried oregano**
- **Salt to taste**

Instructions:

1. In a small bowl, mix paprika, onion powder, garlic powder, thyme, cayenne pepper, black pepper, white pepper, dried oregano, and salt.
2. Rub the spice mixture generously onto both sides of the fish.
3. Allow the rubbed fish to sit for at least 30 minutes to let the flavors penetrate.

4. Grill over medium-high heat until the fish is cooked through, with a delightful Cajun kick.

These flavorful marinades and rubs will elevate your grilled fish to new heights. In the next section, we'll dive into specific recipes for classic grilled fish dishes that showcase these delicious flavor profiles.

Chapter (4) Grilled Fish Recipes

A. Classic Lemon Garlic Grilled Salmon
   Ingredients:

- **4 salmon fillets**
- **1/4 cup olive oil**
- **2 tablespoons fresh lemon juice**
- **3 cloves garlic, minced**
- **1 teaspoon dried oregano**
- **Salt and black pepper to taste**
- **Lemon wedges for serving**

Instructions:

1. In a bowl, whisk together olive oil, lemon juice, minced garlic, dried oregano, salt, and black pepper.
2. Place salmon fillets in a shallow dish and pour the marinade over them, ensuring even coating.
3. Marinate in the refrigerator for at least 30 minutes.
4. Preheat the grill to medium-high heat. Grill salmon for 4-5 minutes per side or until it easily flakes with a fork.
5. Serve with lemon wedges and enjoy.

B. Teriyaki Glazed Grilled Mahi-Mahi
Ingredients:

- **4 mahi-mahi fillets**
- **1/2 cup teriyaki glaze (see Asian-inspired Marinades section)**
- **Sesame seeds for garnish**
- **Green onions, chopped, for garnish**

Instructions:

1. Marinate mahi-mahi fillets in teriyaki glaze for at least 1 hour.
2. Preheat the grill to medium-high heat.
3. Grill mahi-mahi for 4-5 minutes per side, basting with additional teriyaki glaze.
4. Sprinkle sesame seeds and chopped green onions before serving.

C. Cajun-Style Grilled Catfish
Ingredients:

- **4 catfish fillets**
- **Cajun Spice Rub (see Spicy and Bold Rubs section)**
- **2 tablespoons olive oil**
- **Lemon wedges for serving**

Instructions:

1. Rub catfish fillets with Cajun Spice Rub, ensuring thorough coverage.
2. Drizzle olive oil over the fillets and let them sit for at least 30 minutes.
3. Preheat the grill to medium heat.
4. Grill catfish for 4-5 minutes per side or until opaque and easily flaked with a fork.
5. Serve with lemon wedges.

D. Herb-Crusted Grilled Trout
Ingredients:

- **4 trout fillets**
- **Mediterranean Herb Marinade (see Mediterranean Flavors section)**

- 1/2 cup breadcrumbs
- 2 tablespoons fresh parsley, chopped
- Lemon wedges for serving

Instructions:

1. Marinate trout fillets in Mediterranean Herb Marinade for at least 1 hour.
2. Preheat the grill to medium heat.
3. In a bowl, mix breadcrumbs and chopped parsley.
4. Coat the marinated trout fillets with the breadcrumb mixture.
5. Grill for 3-4 minutes per side until the crust is golden and the fish is cooked through.
6. Serve with lemon wedges.

E. Tandoori Spiced Grilled Halibut
Ingredients:

- 4 halibut steaks
- Tandoori Spice Rub (store-bought or see Spicy and Bold Rubs section)
- 1/2 cup plain yogurt
- 2 tablespoons fresh cilantro, chopped
- Lime wedges for serving

Instructions:

1. Rub halibut steaks with Tandoori Spice Rub and let them sit for at least 30 minutes.
2. In a bowl, mix yogurt and chopped cilantro.
3. Preheat the grill to medium-high heat.
4. Grill halibut for 4-5 minutes per side, basting with the yogurt mixture.
5. Serve with lime wedges.

F. Grilled Swordfish with Mango Salsa
Ingredients:

- 4 swordfish steaks
- Salt and black pepper to taste
- Olive oil for brushing

Mango Salsa:

- 1 ripe mango, diced
- 1/2 red onion, finely chopped
- 1 jalapeño, seeded and minced
- 1/4 cup fresh cilantro, chopped
- Juice of 1 lime
- Salt to taste

Instructions:

1. Season swordfish steaks with salt and black pepper, then brush with olive oil.
2. Preheat the grill to medium-high heat.
3. Grill swordfish for 3-4 minutes per side or until grill marks form and the fish is cooked through.
4. In a bowl, combine diced mango, chopped red onion, minced jalapeño, cilantro, lime juice, and salt to make the salsa.
5. Top grilled swordfish with mango salsa before serving.

These grilled fish recipes are designed to showcase a variety of flavors, ensuring a delightful and diverse culinary experience. Feel free to customize them according to your preferences and enjoy the delicious results straight from the grill.

Chapter (5) Sides and Accompaniments

A. Grilled Vegetables
Grilled Lemon Garlic Asparagus:
Ingredients:

- **1 bunch asparagus, trimmed**
- **2 tablespoons olive oil**
- **2 cloves garlic, minced**
- **Zest of 1 lemon**
- **Salt and black pepper to taste**

Instructions:

1. Toss asparagus with olive oil, minced garlic, lemon zest, salt, and black pepper.
2. Grill over medium heat for 5-7 minutes, turning occasionally, until tender and slightly charred.

B. Fresh Salads
Citrus Avocado Salad:
Ingredients:

- **Mixed salad greens**
- **2 ripe avocados, sliced**
- **1 grapefruit, segmented**
- **1 orange, segmented**
- **1/4 cup feta cheese, crumbled**
- **Balsamic vinaigrette dressing**

Instructions:

1. Arrange mixed salad greens on a serving platter.
2. Top with sliced avocados, grapefruit segments, orange

segments, and crumbled feta cheese.

3. Drizzle with balsamic vinaigrette dressing just before serving.

C. Flavored Rice and Quinoa
Lemon Herb Quinoa:
Ingredients:

- **1 cup quinoa, rinsed**
- **2 cups vegetable or chicken broth**
- **Zest of 1 lemon**
- **2 tablespoons fresh parsley, chopped**
- **Salt and black pepper to taste**

Instructions:

1. In a saucepan, bring quinoa and broth to a boil. Reduce heat, cover, and simmer for 15-20 minutes until liquid is absorbed.
2. Fluff quinoa with a fork and stir in lemon zest, chopped parsley, salt, and black pepper.

D. Homemade Sauces and Dips
Garlic Aioli:
Ingredients:

- **1 cup mayonnaise**
- **3 cloves garlic, minced**
- **1 tablespoon lemon juice**
- **Salt and black pepper to taste**

Instructions:

1. In a bowl, combine mayonnaise, minced garlic, lemon juice, salt, and black pepper.
2. Whisk until well blended.
3. Refrigerate for at least 30 minutes before serving to allow flavors to meld.

These sides and accompaniments complement grilled fish perfectly, adding a burst of flavors and textures to your meal. Feel free to mix and match these options to create a well-rounded and satisfying dining experience.

Chapter (6) Tips for Perfect Grilled Fish

A. Monitoring Cooking Times

Know Your Fish: Different types of fish have varying cooking times. Thicker, denser fish like salmon may take longer, while more delicate fish like trout cook more quickly.

Use a Timer: Set a timer to keep track of cooking times, preventing overcooking or undercooking.

Adjust for Thickness: If one piece of fish is thicker than the others, adjust the cooking time accordingly. Thicker cuts generally require more time on the grill.

B. Testing Fish for Doneness

Flake Test: Gently insert a fork into the thickest part of the fish and twist. If the flesh flakes easily and is opaque, the fish is done.

Internal Temperature: Use a meat thermometer to ensure the internal temperature reaches 145°F (63°C) for most fish varieties.

Color and Texture: Grilled fish should have an appealing golden-brown color on the outside and a moist, flaky texture on the inside.

C. Presentation and Garnishes

Fresh Herbs: Garnish grilled fish with freshly chopped herbs like parsley, cilantro, or dill for a burst of color and flavor.

Citrus Wedges: Serve grilled fish with wedges of lemon, lime, or orange on the side. Squeezing citrus over the fish enhances its freshness.

Edible Flowers: For an elegant touch, consider garnishing your grilled fish with edible flowers, such as nasturtiums or pansies.

Sauces and Dips: Drizzle homemade sauces like garlic aioli or serve with a flavorful dip to add an extra layer of taste.

Grilled Lemon Slices: Grill lemon slices alongside the fish for a smoky and caramelized garnish.

Colorful Sides: Arrange vibrant sides, such as the Grilled Lemon Garlic Asparagus or Citrus Avocado Salad, for an appealing and balanced presentation.

Remember, the presentation is not just about aesthetics; it enhances the overall dining experience. With these tips, you'll achieve perfectly grilled fish that not only tastes delicious but also looks impressive on the plate.

Chapter (7) Troubleshooting and FAQs

A. Common Grilling Issues

Fish Sticking to the Grill:

Solution: Ensure the grill grates are well-oiled before placing the fish. Use a grill brush to clean and oil the grates, and consider using a fish basket or foil for delicate varieties.

Dry or Overcooked Fish:

Solution: Monitor cooking times closely. Adjust heat levels and use indirect heat for thicker cuts. Baste with marinade or oil during grilling to retain moisture.

Uneven Cooking:

Solution: Arrange fish fillets with similar thickness on the grill. If using a charcoal grill, distribute the charcoal evenly. Rotate or rearrange fish if needed during cooking.

Fish Falling Apart:

Solution: Handle delicate fish with care. Use a spatula for flipping, and consider grilling on cedar planks or in foil packets to maintain structure.

Excessive Smoke:
Solution: Clean the grill grates to remove excess residue. Ensure the drip tray is empty. Soak wood chips before adding them for smoking to control the intensity.

B. Frequently Asked Questions
How long should I marinate the fish?
Answer: Marinate fish for at least 30 minutes to allow flavors to penetrate. For a more intense flavor, you can marinate for up to 24 hours in the refrigerator.

What is the best way to thaw frozen fish for grilling?
Answer: Thaw fish in the refrigerator overnight for even thawing. Alternatively, use the defrost function on your microwave or place the sealed fish in a bowl of cold water.

Can I grill fish directly from the freezer?
Answer: While possible, it's better to thaw fish before grilling for even cooking. Grilling frozen fish may result in uneven cooking and a less desirable texture.

What's the best method for cleaning the grill grates?
Answer: Preheat the grill and use a grill brush to scrub away residue. For stubborn build-up, consider using a crumpled piece of aluminum foil or a specialized grill cleaner.

How do I prevent flare-ups during grilling?
Answer: Trim excess fat from fish to reduce flare-ups. Keep a spray bottle of water nearby to extinguish flames if necessary. Ensure the drip tray is clean and positioned correctly.

These troubleshooting tips and FAQs address common concerns during the grilling process, ensuring a smoother and more enjoyable experience for both novice and experienced grillers.

Chapter (8) Beyond the Grill

A. Leftover Fish Ideas

Fish Tacos:

Flake leftover grilled fish and use it as a filling for tacos. Top with shredded cabbage, salsa, and a drizzle of lime crema.

Fish Salad:

Toss grilled fish with mixed greens, cherry tomatoes, cucumber, and your favorite salad dressing for a refreshing leftover meal.

Fish Sandwich:

Layer grilled fish between slices of bread or in a bun with lettuce, tomato, and your choice of condiments for a quick and satisfying sandwich.

Fish Wrap:

Wrap leftover grilled fish in a tortilla with hummus, greens, and roasted vegetables for a flavorful and portable lunch.

Fish Pasta:

Incorporate flaked grilled fish into a pasta dish with your preferred sauce, vegetables, and herbs for a simple and tasty pasta creation.

B. Freezing and Reheating Grilled Fish

Freezing:

Allow grilled fish to cool completely before freezing. Wrap the fish tightly in plastic wrap or aluminum foil. Place in an airtight container or a resealable plastic bag. Label with the date and freeze for up to 2-3 months.

Reheating:

Thaw frozen grilled fish in the refrigerator overnight. Reheat in a preheated oven at 350°F (180°C) for about 10-15 minutes or until warmed through. Alternatively, gently reheat in a skillet over medium heat with a splash of water to retain moisture.

C. Complementary Beverages

Citrus Infused Water:

Create a refreshing beverage by infusing water with slices of lemon, lime, and orange. Add mint leaves for an extra burst of flavor.

Iced Herbal Tea:

Brew a pot of herbal tea such as mint, chamomile, or hibiscus, then chill it and serve over ice for a cooling and caffeine-free option.

Cucumber Lime Sparkler:

Mix cucumber slices, lime juice, and a splash of sparkling water for a light and hydrating beverage.

Ginger Lemonade:

Make a zesty ginger lemonade by combining freshly squeezed lemon juice, ginger syrup, and cold water. Serve over ice.

White Sangria:

Prepare a white sangria with white wine, sliced peaches, berries, and a splash of sparkling water for a fruity and festive option.

These ideas extend the enjoyment of grilled fish beyond the initial meal, providing creative ways to repurpose leftovers and offering refreshing beverage options to accompany your seafood dishes.

Chapter (9) Global Grilling Adventures

A. Caribbean Jerk Spiced Grilled Red Snapper
Ingredients:

- 4 red snapper fillets
- 1/4 cup Caribbean jerk seasoning
- 2 tablespoons olive oil
- 2 tablespoons lime juice
- Fresh cilantro for garnish

Instructions:

1. Rub red snapper fillets with Caribbean jerk seasoning, ensuring even coverage.
2. Mix olive oil and lime juice, then brush the mixture over the seasoned fish.
3. Preheat the grill to medium-high heat and grill snapper for 4-5 minutes per side or until done.
4. Garnish with fresh cilantro before serving.

B. Greek-Style Grilled Branzino
Ingredients:

- 2 whole branzino, gutted and scaled
- 1/4 cup extra-virgin olive oil
- 2 tablespoons fresh lemon juice
- 3 cloves garlic, minced
- 1 teaspoon dried oregano
- Salt and black pepper to taste
- Lemon wedges for serving

Instructions:

1. Score both sides of branzino with diagonal cuts.
2. In a bowl, whisk together olive oil, lemon juice, minced garlic, dried oregano, salt, and black pepper.
3. Brush the fish with the marinade, inside and out.
4. Grill over medium heat for 5-7 minutes per side until the skin is crispy and the flesh is flaky.
5. Serve with lemon wedges.

C. Brazilian Chimichurri Grilled Tilapia
Ingredients:

- **4 tilapia fillets**
- **Chimichurri Sauce:**
- **1 cup fresh parsley, chopped**
- **1/4 cup fresh cilantro, chopped**
- **3 cloves garlic, minced**
- **1/2 cup extra-virgin olive oil**
- **2 tablespoons red wine vinegar**
- **1 teaspoon dried oregano**
- **Salt and black pepper to taste**

Instructions:

1. Combine all chimichurri sauce ingredients in a blender or food processor until well-blended.
2. Marinate tilapia fillets in half of the chimichurri sauce for at least 30 minutes.
3. Preheat the grill to medium-high heat and grill tilapia for 3-4 minutes per side.
4. Drizzle remaining chimichurri sauce over the grilled fish before serving.

D. Thai Coconut Lemongrass Grilled Sea Bass
Ingredients:

- **4 sea bass fillets**
- **1/2 cup coconut milk**
- **2 tablespoons fish sauce**
- **1 tablespoon lemongrass, minced**
- **1 tablespoon fresh lime juice**
- **1 teaspoon brown sugar**
- **Fresh cilantro and lime wedges for garnish**

Instructions:

1. In a bowl, whisk together coconut milk, fish sauce, lemongrass, lime juice, and brown sugar.
2. Marinate sea bass fillets in the mixture for at least 1 hour.
3. Preheat the grill to medium heat and grill sea bass for 4-5 minutes per side.
4. Garnish with fresh cilantro and serve with lime wedges.

E. Moroccan Harissa Grilled Swordfish
Ingredients:

- **4 swordfish steaks**
- **Harissa Marinade:**
- **2 tablespoons harissa paste**
- **2 tablespoons olive oil**
- **1 tablespoon lemon juice**
- **1 teaspoon ground cumin**
- **1 teaspoon ground coriander**
- **Salt and black pepper to taste**

Instructions:

1. Mix harissa paste, olive oil, lemon juice, cumin, coriander, salt, and black pepper to make the marinade.
2. Coat swordfish steaks with the harissa marinade and let them marinate for at least 30 minutes.
3. Preheat the grill to medium-high heat and grill swordfish for 3-4 minutes per side or until done.
4. Serve the grilled swordfish steaks with your favorite side dishes.

Embark on a global grilling adventure with these diverse and flavorful recipes that showcase the culinary richness of different regions. Enjoy the unique taste experiences each dish offers!

Chapter (10) Creative Seafood Fusion

A. Wasabi Sesame Grilled Tuna Steaks
   Ingredients:

- 4 tuna steaks
- 2 tablespoons soy sauce
- 1 tablespoon sesame oil
- 1 tablespoon rice vinegar
- 1 tablespoon honey
- 1 tablespoon fresh lime juice
- 1 tablespoon wasabi paste
- 1 tablespoon sesame seeds
- Green onions for garnish

Instructions:

1. In a bowl, whisk together soy sauce, sesame oil, rice vinegar, honey, lime juice, and wasabi paste to create the marinade.
2. Coat tuna steaks with the marinade and let them marinate for 30 minutes.
3. Preheat the grill to high heat and grill tuna for 1-2 minutes per side.
4. Sprinkle sesame seeds and garnish with sliced green onions before serving.

B. Pesto and Sun-Dried Tomato Stuffed Grilled Trout
Ingredients:

- **4 trout fillets**
- **Pesto Sauce:**
- **2 cups fresh basil leaves**
- **1/2 cup pine nuts**
- **1/2 cup grated Parmesan cheese**
- **2 cloves garlic**
- **1/2 cup extra-virgin olive oil**
- **Salt and black pepper to taste**
- **Sun-dried tomatoes, chopped**

Instructions:

1. In a food processor, combine basil, pine nuts, Parmesan, garlic, and olive oil to make the pesto sauce. Season with salt and black pepper.
2. Spread pesto on one side of each trout fillet and sprinkle chopped sun-dried tomatoes on top.
3. Fold the fillets in half, securing the filling.
4. Preheat the grill to medium heat and grill trout for 3-4 minutes per side or until cooked through.

C. Mexican Street Corn Grilled Fish Tacos
Ingredients:

- **1 lb white fish fillets (tilapia or cod)**
- **1 cup Mexican street corn (corn, mayo, cotija cheese, chili**

powder)
- **Corn tortillas**
- **Lime wedges**
- **Fresh cilantro for garnish**

Instructions:

1. Grill white fish fillets over medium heat for 3-4 minutes per side or until flaky.
2. Warm corn tortillas on the grill.
3. Spread Mexican street corn mixture on each tortilla, top with grilled fish, and garnish with fresh cilantro.
4. Serve with lime wedges.

D. Teriyaki Pineapple Grilled Salmon Skewers
Ingredients:

- **1 lb salmon fillets, cut into cubes**
- **1 cup pineapple chunks**
- **Teriyaki Marinade:**
- **1/4 cup soy sauce**
- **2 tablespoons honey**
- **1 tablespoon rice vinegar**
- **1 tablespoon mirin (Japanese sweet rice wine)**
- **1 teaspoon grated ginger**
- **2 cloves garlic, minced**

Instructions:

1. In a bowl, mix soy sauce, honey, rice vinegar, mirin, ginger, and minced garlic to create the teriyaki marinade.
2. Thread salmon cubes and pineapple chunks onto skewers.
3. Brush skewers with teriyaki marinade and grill over medium-high heat for 3-4 minutes per side or until salmon is cooked

through.

E. Grilled Fish Banh Mi Sandwiches
Ingredients:

- **4 white fish fillets (such as snapper or cod)**
- **Baguettes or sandwich rolls**
- **Pickled daikon and carrot slaw**
- **Fresh cucumber slices**
- **Fresh cilantro leaves**
- **Sriracha mayo:**
- **1/2 cup mayonnaise**
- **2 tablespoons Sriracha sauce**
- **1 tablespoon lime juice**

Instructions:

1. Grill white fish fillets over medium heat for 3-4 minutes per side or until flaky.
2. Mix mayonnaise, Sriracha, and lime juice to create the Sriracha mayo.
3. Assemble sandwiches with grilled fish, pickled slaw, cucumber slices, cilantro, and a drizzle of Sriracha mayo.
4. Serve immediately.

These creative seafood fusion recipes bring together diverse flavors and ingredients to create exciting and delicious dishes that go beyond traditional boundaries. Enjoy exploring new taste combinations!

Chapter (11) Health-Conscious Grilling

A. Grilled Fish with Superfood Quinoa Salad
   Grilled Fish:

- 4 fish fillets (such as salmon or trout)
- Olive oil for brushing
- Lemon wedges for serving

Superfood Quinoa Salad:

- 1 cup quinoa, cooked and cooled
- 1 cup cherry tomatoes, halved
- 1 cucumber, diced
- 1/2 cup feta cheese, crumbled
- 1/4 cup Kalamata olives, sliced
- 2 tablespoons extra-virgin olive oil
- 2 tablespoons balsamic vinegar
- Salt and black pepper to taste
- Fresh basil leaves for garnish

Instructions:

1. Brush fish fillets with olive oil and grill over medium heat for 4-5 minutes per side or until cooked through.
2. In a bowl, combine quinoa, cherry tomatoes, cucumber, feta, and olives.
3. Whisk together olive oil, balsamic vinegar, salt, and black pepper. Drizzle over the quinoa salad and toss.
4. Serve grilled fish over a bed of superfood quinoa salad, garnished with fresh basil leaves and lemon wedges.

B. Mediterranean Grilled Mackerel with Olive Tapenade

Ingredients:

- **4 mackerel fillets**
- **Olive oil for brushing**
- **Lemon wedges for serving**

Olive Tapenade:
1 cup Kalamata olives, pitted
2 tablespoons capers
2 cloves garlic, minced
2 tablespoons fresh parsley, chopped
2 tablespoons extra-virgin olive oil
1 tablespoon lemon juice
Instructions:

1. Brush mackerel fillets with olive oil and grill over medium-high heat for 3-4 minutes per side.
2. In a food processor, pulse olives, capers, garlic, parsley, olive oil, and lemon juice until coarsely chopped.
3. Serve grilled mackerel topped with olive tapenade and lemon wedges.

C. Grilled Rainbow Trout with Avocado Salsa
Ingredients:

- 4 rainbow trout fillets
- Olive oil for brushing
- Lime wedges for serving

Avocado Salsa:

- 2 avocados, diced
- 1 cup cherry tomatoes, diced
- 1/4 cup red onion, finely chopped
- 1/4 cup fresh cilantro, chopped
- 1 jalapeño, seeded and minced
- 2 tablespoons lime juice
- Salt and black pepper to taste

Instructions:

1. Brush rainbow trout fillets with olive oil and grill over medium heat for 3-4 minutes per side.
2. In a bowl, combine diced avocados, cherry tomatoes, red onion, cilantro, jalapeño, lime juice, salt, and black pepper.
3. Top grilled trout with avocado salsa and serve with lime wedges.

D. Herb-Infused Grilled Haddock with Steamed Vegetables
Ingredients:

- 4 haddock fillets
- Olive oil for brushing
- Fresh herbs (rosemary, thyme, or dill), chopped
- Lemon wedges for serving

Steamed Vegetables:

- **2 cups mixed vegetables (broccoli, carrots, and snap peas)**
- **1 tablespoon olive oil**
- **Salt and black pepper to taste**

Instructions:

1. Brush haddock fillets with olive oil and sprinkle with chopped fresh herbs. Grill over medium heat for 4-5 minutes per side.
2. Steam mixed vegetables until tender-crisp. Toss with olive oil, salt, and black pepper.
3. Serve grilled haddock over a bed of steamed vegetables with lemon wedges.

E. Grilled Sardines on a Bed of Quinoa and Spinach

Ingredients:

- **8 fresh sardines, cleaned and gutted**
- **Olive oil for brushing**
- **Lemon wedges for serving**

Quinoa and Spinach Bed:

- **1 cup quinoa, cooked and cooled**
- **2 cups fresh spinach, chopped**
- **1 tablespoon olive oil**
- **1 tablespoon balsamic vinegar**
- **Salt and black pepper to taste**

Instructions:

1. Brush sardines with olive oil and grill over medium-high heat for 2-3 minutes per side.
2. In a bowl, mix quinoa, chopped spinach, olive oil, balsamic

vinegar, salt, and black pepper.
3. Serve grilled sardines on a bed of quinoa and spinach, accompanied by lemon wedges.

These health-conscious grilling recipes incorporate nutrient-rich ingredients and lean protein sources, providing a delicious and wholesome dining experience. Enjoy these flavorful dishes that prioritize both taste and well-being!

Chapter (12) eafood and Wine Pairing

A. Choosing the Right Wine for Grilled Fish

Grilled fish offers a versatile canvas for wine pairing, and your choice can enhance the overall dining experience. Consider the following recommendations:

Sauvignon Blanc: This crisp white wine complements the light and flaky texture of grilled fish. Its citrusy and herbal notes work well with dishes featuring lemon, herbs, or lighter marinades.

Chardonnay: A medium to full-bodied Chardonnay can pair beautifully with grilled fish, especially if it's rich and buttery. Opt for unoaked or lightly oaked Chardonnays to avoid overwhelming delicate fish flavors.

Pinot Grigio: This refreshing white wine offers a balanced acidity that pairs well with grilled fish, particularly those with minimal seasoning. It's an excellent choice for more subtly flavored dishes.

Rosé: A dry rosé, with its vibrant and fruity profile, can be a delightful companion to grilled fish. Choose a Provencal or Spanish rosé for a crisp and refreshing pairing.

Champagne or Sparkling Wine: For special occasions, the effervescence of Champagne or sparkling wine can elevate the dining experience, especially when paired with grilled shellfish.

Albariño: Hailing from Spain, Albariño's bright acidity and citrus notes make it a great match for grilled seafood, particularly dishes with a hint of spice.

B. Wine Marinades and Glazes

Enhance the flavors of your grilled fish with wine-infused marinades and glazes:

White Wine Lemon Herb Marinade:

Combine Sauvignon Blanc, lemon juice, minced garlic, fresh herbs (such as thyme and parsley), and olive oil for a light and aromatic marinade.

Chardonnay Dijon Glaze:

Mix Chardonnay, Dijon mustard, honey, and a touch of melted butter for a rich and savory glaze perfect for basting grilled salmon or trout.

Rosé Citrus Glaze:

Create a vibrant glaze using rosé, orange juice, honey, and a pinch of red pepper flakes for a sweet and slightly spicy kick.

C. Wine-Infused Seafood Sauces

Elevate your grilled seafood with these wine-infused sauces:

Sauvignon Blanc Cilantro Chimichurri:

Blend Sauvignon Blanc, fresh cilantro, garlic, olive oil, and red wine vinegar for a zesty chimichurri to drizzle over grilled shrimp or fish.

Pinot Grigio Lemon Butter Sauce:

Simmer Pinot Grigio with lemon juice, capers, and butter for a luxurious sauce that complements the richness of grilled scallops or halibut.

Champagne Mango Salsa:

Combine Champagne, diced mango, red onion, cilantro, and lime juice for a refreshing salsa to top grilled swordfish or tuna.

D. Tips for Hosting a Grilled Fish and Wine Pairing Dinner

Consider the Intensity: Match lighter wines with milder fish, and more robust wines with stronger-flavored fish or richer preparations.

Balance Flavors: Choose wines that balance or enhance the flavors of your grilled seafood. Citrusy wines work well with lemony or herbed dishes, while buttery Chardonnays complement richer flavors.

Experiment with Sparkling Wines: Sparkling wines, including Champagne, can be surprisingly versatile with grilled seafood. The bubbles cut through the richness and provide a festive touch.

Temperature Matters: Serve white wines chilled but not overly cold, as extreme cold can mute the flavors. Reds can be slightly chilled, especially in warmer weather.

Provide Variety: Offer a selection of wines to cater to different preferences. Include at least one white, one rosé, and one red option to accommodate various grilled seafood dishes.

Hosting a grilled fish and wine pairing dinner can be a delightful experience, allowing guests to explore the harmony between different wines and seafood flavors.

Chapter (13) Grilling for Special Occasions

A. Grilled Fish for Summer Barbecues
Grilled Citrus Salmon Skewers:
Ingredients:

- **Salmon cubes**
- **Bell peppers, onions, and cherry tomatoes**
- **Marinade: Olive oil, lemon juice, garlic, dill, salt, and black pepper**

Instructions:

1. Marinate salmon cubes and vegetables in the olive oil, lemon juice, garlic, dill, salt, and black pepper mixture for 30 minutes.
2. Thread salmon and veggies onto skewers.
3. Grill over medium-high heat for 3-4 minutes per side.
4. Serve with a refreshing cucumber and mint yogurt sauce.

B. Elegant Grilled Seafood Platters for Dinner Parties
Grilled Seafood Platter:

- **Assorted seafood (shrimp, scallops, lobster tails, and squid)**
- **Marinade: Olive oil, garlic, lemon zest, fresh herbs (rosemary, thyme, parsley), salt, and black pepper**

Instructions:

1. Marinate seafood in the olive oil, garlic, lemon zest, fresh herbs, salt, and black pepper mixture for 1 hour.
2. Grill each type of seafood separately to ensure proper cooking

times.

3. Arrange grilled seafood on a platter and garnish with additional fresh herbs.
4. Serve with a selection of dipping sauces like aioli, chimichurri, and lemon butter.

C. Grilled Fish for Holiday Feasts
Herb-Roasted Grilled Branzino:
Ingredients:

- **Whole branzino, gutted and scaled**
- **Marinade: Olive oil, lemon juice, garlic, rosemary, thyme, salt, and black pepper**

Instructions:

1. Make deep cuts on both sides of the branzino.
2. Mix olive oil, lemon juice, minced garlic, chopped rosemary, thyme, salt, and black pepper for the marinade.
3. Rub the marinade onto the branzino, including inside the cavity.
4. Grill over medium heat for 8-10 minutes per side or until the skin is crispy and the flesh is flaky.
5. Serve the whole grilled branzino on a festive platter.

D. Romantic Grilled Seafood Dinner for Two
Grilled Lobster Tails with Garlic Butter:
Ingredients:

- **Lobster tails, split**
- **Marinade: Olive oil, garlic, fresh parsley, lemon juice, salt, and black pepper**

- **Garlic butter for serving**

Instructions:

1. Marinate split lobster tails in a mixture of olive oil, minced garlic, chopped fresh parsley, lemon juice, salt, and black pepper for 30 minutes.
2. Grill lobster tails flesh side down over medium-high heat for 4-5 minutes.
3. Flip and continue grilling for an additional 4-5 minutes or until the lobster is opaque and cooked through.
4. Serve with a side of melted garlic butter for dipping.
5. Accompany with grilled asparagus and a bottle of Champagne for a romantic touch.

These grilled fish recipes are designed to add a touch of elegance and flavor to special occasions, whether it's a summer barbecue, a dinner party, a holiday feast, or a romantic dinner for two. Enjoy the festivities and the delightful flavors of grilled seafood!

Chapter (14) Grilled Fish for Kids

A. Family-Friendly Grilled Fish Recipes
Cheesy Grilled Fish Tacos:
Ingredients:

- Mild white fish fillets
- Taco seasoning
- Shredded cheese
- Mini tortillas
- Toppings: Shredded lettuce, diced tomatoes, and mild salsa

Instructions:

1. Season fish fillets with taco seasoning.
2. Grill over medium heat for 3-4 minutes per side.
3. Place grilled fish in mini tortillas, top with cheese, lettuce, tomatoes, and salsa.

Fish and Veggie Skewers:
Ingredients:

- Bite-sized fish chunks
- Cherry tomatoes
- Bell pepper chunks
- Zucchini slices
- Olive oil, lemon juice, and herbs for marinade

Instructions:

1. Marinade fish and veggies in a mixture of olive oil, lemon juice, and herbs.
2. Thread onto skewers and grill for 3-4 minutes per side.

B. Creative Fish Shapes and Skewers
Fish Shapes on the Grill:
Use fish-shaped molds to shape fish patties. Grill until cooked through, creating fun and appealing fish-shaped servings for kids.
Rainbow Fish Skewers:
Thread colorful veggies (cherry tomatoes, bell peppers, and zucchini) and fish chunks onto skewers. Grill for a vibrant and playful meal.
C. Involving Kids in the Grilling Process
Build-Your-Own Fish Tacos:
Set up a taco station with grilled fish, tortillas, and a variety of toppings. Allow kids to assemble their own tacos for a hands-on experience.
Vegetable Skewer Creations:
Let kids choose their favorite veggies to thread onto skewers alongside fish. Encourage creativity and personalization.
D. Tips for Picky Eaters
Mild Flavors:
Opt for mild white fish varieties like cod or haddock. Mild-flavored fish is often more appealing to picky eaters.
Fun Presentation:
Create visually appealing presentations, such as arranging fish in creative shapes or using colorful skewers. Fun presentations can make the meal more enticing for kids.
Dipping Sauces:
Offer a variety of kid-friendly dipping sauces like yogurt-based ranch or a mild salsa. Having dipping options can make the meal more interactive.
Grilled Fruit Sides:
Include grilled fruit as a side, such as pineapple or watermelon. The sweetness can balance the savory flavors and appeal to children's taste buds.

Let Them Choose:

Involve kids in the decision-making process by letting them choose the type of fish, marinade, or even the veggies for skewers. Having a say in the meal can increase their interest.

Grilled fish for kids can be a delightful and interactive experience. By incorporating creative shapes, involving kids in the process, and making the meal visually appealing, you can make grilled fish a favorite among young eaters.

Chapter (15) Vegetarian Grilling with a Seafood Twist

A. Grilled Portobello Mushrooms Stuffed with Crab

Ingredients:

- Portobello mushrooms, stems removed
- Lump crab meat
- Cream cheese
- Garlic, minced
- Fresh parsley, chopped
- Lemon juice
- Salt and black pepper to taste
- Olive oil for grilling

Instructions:

1. Preheat the grill to medium-high heat.
2. In a bowl, mix crab meat, cream cheese, minced garlic, chopped parsley, lemon juice, salt, and black pepper.
3. Fill the portobello mushrooms with the crab mixture.
4. Brush the mushrooms with olive oil and grill for 6-8 minutes until mushrooms are tender and the filling is heated through.
5. Serve as a savory appetizer or a flavorful side dish.

B. Grilled Stuffed Bell Peppers with Shrimp
Ingredients:

- Bell peppers, halved and seeds removed
- Shrimp, peeled and deveined
- Quinoa, cooked
- Cherry tomatoes, halved
- Red onion, finely chopped
- Feta cheese, crumbled
- Fresh basil, chopped
- Olive oil for grilling
- Balsamic glaze for drizzling

Instructions:

1. Preheat the grill to medium heat.
2. In a bowl, mix cooked quinoa, cherry tomatoes, red onion, feta cheese, and fresh basil.
3. Stuff each bell pepper half with the quinoa mixture and top with shrimp.
4. Brush the peppers with olive oil and grill for 10-12 minutes or until the shrimp are cooked.
5. Drizzle with balsamic glaze before serving.

C. Grilled Eggplant and Tomato Seafood Towers
Ingredients:

- **Eggplant, sliced into rounds**
- **Large tomatoes, sliced**
- **Avocado, sliced**
- **Cucumber, sliced**
- **Smoked salmon**
- **Cream cheese**
- **Capers**
- **Fresh dill**
- **Olive oil for grilling**

Instructions:

1. Preheat the grill to medium-high heat.
2. Brush eggplant slices with olive oil and grill for 3-4 minutes per side until tender.
3. Assemble towers by layering grilled eggplant, tomato slices, avocado, cucumber, and smoked salmon.
4. Top each tower with a dollop of cream cheese, capers, and fresh dill.
5. Serve these seafood-inspired towers as a light and refreshing appetizer.

D. Tofu and Seaweed Skewers with Teriyaki Glaze
Ingredients:

- **Firm tofu, cubed**
- **Seaweed sheets, cut into strips**
- **Teriyaki glaze:**
- **Soy sauce**
- **Mirin (Japanese sweet rice wine)**
- **Brown sugar**
- **Garlic, minced**
- **Ginger, grated**

Instructions:

1. Preheat the grill to medium heat.
2. Thread tofu cubes and seaweed strips onto skewers.
3. In a small saucepan, combine soy sauce, mirin, brown sugar, minced garlic, and grated ginger to make the teriyaki glaze.
4. Grill the skewers for 3-4 minutes per side, brushing with teriyaki glaze during cooking.
5. Serve these flavorful skewers with a side of rice or a crisp salad.

These vegetarian grilling recipes with a seafood twist offer a creative and satisfying alternative for those looking to enjoy the essence of seafood while embracing a plant-based approach. Enjoy the delicious flavors and textures these dishes bring to your grilling experience!

Chapter (16) The Art of Grilled Seafood Desserts

A. Grilled Pineapple with Honey and Lime
Ingredients:

- **Pineapple slices, cored**
- **Honey**
- **Lime zest**
- **Fresh mint leaves for garnish**

Instructions:

1. Preheat the grill to medium-high heat.
2. Grill pineapple slices for 2-3 minutes per side or until grill marks appear.
3. Drizzle grilled pineapple with honey and sprinkle with lime zest.
4. Garnish with fresh mint leaves and serve warm.

B. Coconut-Lime Grilled Peaches with Mint
Ingredients:

- **Ripe peaches, halved and pitted**
- **Coconut oil, melted**
- **Lime juice**
- **Shredded coconut**
- **Fresh mint leaves for garnish**

Instructions:

1. Preheat the grill to medium heat.

2. Brush peach halves with melted coconut oil and grill for 3-4 minutes per side.
3. Drizzle grilled peaches with lime juice and sprinkle shredded coconut on top.
4. Garnish with fresh mint leaves before serving.

C. Grilled Banana Foster with Rum-Infused Syrup
Ingredients:

- **Bananas, halved lengthwise**
- **Butter**
- **Brown sugar**
- **Cinnamon**
- **Dark rum**
- **Vanilla ice cream (optional)**

Instructions:

1. In a small saucepan, melt butter, brown sugar, and cinnamon over low heat until a syrup forms.
2. Place banana halves on the grill over medium heat for 2-3 minutes per side.
3. Drizzle the rum-infused syrup over the grilled bananas.
4. Optionally, serve over vanilla ice cream for a decadent treat.

D. Grilled Chocolate-Drizzled Fruit Kebabs
Ingredients:

- **Assorted fruits (strawberries, pineapple chunks, banana slices)**
- **Dark chocolate, melted**
- **Chopped nuts (walnuts, almonds) for coating**

1. **Instructions:**
2. Preheat the grill to medium-high heat.
3. Thread assorted fruits onto skewers.
4. Grill fruit kebabs for 2-3 minutes per side.
5. Drizzle melted dark chocolate over the grilled fruit and roll in chopped nuts.
6. Serve immediately for a delightful and indulgent grilled dessert.

These grilled seafood desserts offer a unique twist to your sweet cravings. The combination of grilled fruits, flavorful sauces, and creative toppings creates a memorable ending to any barbecue or outdoor gathering. Enjoy the art of grilling with these delicious and inventive dessert ideas!

Chapter (17) Grilling Mastery Beyond Fish

A. Grilled Seafood Paella

Elevate your grilling expertise with the rich flavors of a classic Grilled Seafood Paella. Learn the art of creating the perfect socarrat (crispy rice crust) while infusing your favorite seafood, saffron, and smoky goodness from the grill.

B. Surf and Turf Grilling Techniques

Master the balance of land and sea with Surf and Turf Grilling Techniques. Discover the secrets of perfectly grilling succulent steaks and seafood, creating a symphony of flavors that will impress even the most discerning palates.

C. Seafood Grilled Pizza

Take pizza night to a whole new level by mastering the art of Seafood Grilled Pizza. Learn the techniques for achieving a perfectly crispy crust on the grill, and explore inventive seafood toppings that will turn your backyard into a pizzeria.

D. Grilled Seafood Appetizer Platter

Impress your guests with a Grilled Seafood Appetizer Platter that showcases your grilling mastery. Explore a variety of appetizers featuring grilled shrimp, calamari, and more, arranged artfully for a show-stopping display.

Whether you're delving into the complexities of Grilled Seafood Paella, mastering the art of Surf and Turf, experimenting with Seafood Grilled Pizza, or creating a stunning Grilled Seafood Appetizer Platter, these recipes will take your grilling expertise to new heights. Enjoy the diverse and delectable world of grilling beyond fish!

Chapter (18) Grilling Fish for Breakfast

A. Smoked Salmon and Cream Cheese Bagels on the Grill

Wake up to a gourmet breakfast with Smoked Salmon and Cream Cheese Bagels on the Grill. Explore the art of infusing smoky flavors into delicate salmon, served on a perfectly grilled bagel with a generous smear of cream cheese. A breakfast delight that's both sophisticated and satisfying.

B. Grilled Fish Breakfast Burritos

Start your day with a protein-packed Grilled Fish Breakfast Burrito. Master the art of grilling fish fillets to perfection, then wrap them in a tortilla with scrambled eggs, salsa, and your favorite toppings. A hearty and flavorful breakfast on the grill.

C. Grilled Tuna and Egg Breakfast Skillet

Elevate your breakfast routine with a Grilled Tuna and Egg Breakfast Skillet. Learn the techniques of grilling tuna to a succulent finish, then combine it with perfectly cooked eggs and your favorite veggies for a skillet that's both nutritious and delicious.

D. Grilled Sardines with Toasted Bread and Avocado

Experience a Mediterranean-inspired breakfast with Grilled Sardines, Toasted Bread, and Avocado. Master the art of grilling sardines to achieve a smoky flavor, then serve them on toasted bread with creamy avocado for a delightful and wholesome morning meal.

Whether you're savoring Smoked Salmon and Cream Cheese Bagels, indulging in Grilled Fish Breakfast Burritos, enjoying a Grilled Tuna and Egg Breakfast Skillet, or embracing the Mediterranean flavors of Grilled Sardines, these breakfast recipes will make your mornings unforgettable. Grilling fish for breakfast has never been this delicious!

Conclusion

A. Celebrating Successes

As you embark on your journey into the world of mastering grilled fish, take a moment to savor the successes and accomplishments you've achieved. Celebrate the delicious flavors, the enticing aromas, and the joy that grilling brings to your culinary adventures. Whether you've perfected a classic recipe or ventured into creative and global flavors, each success is a testament to your passion for the art of grilling.

B. Encouragement for Continued Grilling Mastery

The journey of grilling is a continuous exploration of flavors, techniques, and culinary creativity. As you continue your grilling mastery, embrace the opportunity to try new recipes, experiment with diverse marinades, and elevate your skills with each session at the grill. There's always more to discover, whether it's perfecting the art of indirect heat, delving into unique global recipes, or crafting your own signature marinades.

Remember, the essence of grilling is not just about the food on the plate but the experiences shared around the grill. It's about creating moments of joy, laughter, and connection with family and friends. So, keep the flames alive, the grill sizzling, and your culinary curiosity burning. May your future grilling endeavors be filled with delicious discoveries and the satisfaction of a well-grilled masterpiece.

Happy grilling, and may your culinary journey be as vibrant and flavorful as the dishes you create!

www.ingramcontent.com/pod-product-compliance
Lightning Source LLC
Chambersburg PA
CBHW031126160726
47989CB00016B/1803